Be Who You Are

By Aaron Fields

Copyright © 2021 Aaron Fields. All rights reserved.

Published by The Write Perspective, LLC

Dallas, Texas,

All rights reserved. No part of this book shall be reproduced or transmitted in any form or by any means, electronic, mechanical, magnetic, photographic including photocopying, recording or by any information storage and retrieval system, without prior written permission of the publisher. No copyright liability is assumed with respect to the use of the information contained in this book. Even though every precaution has been taken in preparation of this book, the publisher/author assumes no responsibility for errors or omissions. Neither is any liability assumed for any damage that results from the use of the information in this book.

ISBN: 978-1-953962-40-9

When you have problems with your own self-image, you'll take on the persona of another person.

Aaron Fields

Being who you are is important, being someone else is not cool.

Being someone else is unhealthy, being yourself means you rule.

Admire and appreciate their gifts, but don't be a fan.

Focus on your own gifts, I know you can.

Don't lose who you are, don't become obsess.

Be who you are, create your own success

Don't insult yourself, overcome envy.

When you have no identity, you become empty.

It's okay to love yourself, I know you do.

I'm satisfied with who I am, what about you?

Remain peaceful and happy, don't steal the other person's place.

Why copy off of others, when you can create your own space.

Food For Thought

Trying to be like someone else means you're not appreciating yourself and your own identity.

Don't assume the role of another person, just be who you are.

Don't be afraid to let your life and your gifts shine.

Knowing who you are can lead to a peaceful life.

Expect greatness out of yourself

Live up to your own standards as oppose to being like someone else.

Always pursue knowledge and information.

You don't have to be like everyone else.

Tips

Having the ability of knowing who you are will help you make better decisions to achieve higher goals.

- Take a closer look at yourself and figure out what is it that you like and don't like
- Write down your strengths and weaknesses
- Start asking yourself Important questions
- Don't be afraid of failing and make sure you grow and learn from your mistakes
- Stay persistent
- Don't let your failure cause you to lose sight of your goals.